Christmas Songs and Carols
for Classical Singers

Low Voice

To access companion recorded accompaniments online, visit:
www.halleonard.com/mylibrary

Enter Code
2503-9265-7298-5114

Cover painting: Agnes Tait, *Skating in Central Park*, 1934

ISBN 978-1-4950-9851-2

7777 W. BLUEMOUND RD. P.O. BOX 13819 MILWAUKEE, WI 53213

Visit Hal Leonard Online at
www.halleonard.com

Contents

Pianists on the recordings: [1] Brian Dean, [2] Brendan Fox, [3] Richard Walters

Christmas Time Is Here
from A CHARLIE BROWN CHRISTMAS

Words by Lee Mendelson
Music by Vince Guaraldi
Arranged by Joshua Parman

Christ-mas time is here, hap-pi-ness and cheer. Fun for all that chil-dren call their fa-v'rite time of year.

Snow-flakes in the air, car-ols ev-'ry-where, old-en times and an-cient rhymes of love and dreams to share.

Sleigh-bells in the air, beau-ty ev-'ry-

where.   Yule-tide by   the   fi - re-side   and joy-ful mem - 'ries   there.

Christ-mas time   is   here,   we'll be draw -   ing

near.   Oh, that we   could al - ways see   such spir - it through the

year.

The Christmas Song
(Chestnuts Roasting on an Open Fire)

Music and Lyric by Mel Tormé
and Robert Wells
Arranged by Richard Walters

help to make the sea - son bright. Ti - ny tots with their

eyes all a - glow will find it hard to sleep to - night. They __ know that

San - ta's __ on his way; he's __ load - ed lots of toys __ and good - ies __ on his

sleigh, and __ ev - 'ry mother's child _____ is __ gon - na spy to __ see if

rein - deer __ real - ly know how to fly And so I'm of - fer - ing this

sim - ple phrase __ to kids from one to __ nine - ty - two, al -

though __ it's been said __ man - y times man - y ways, Mer - ry Christ - mas,

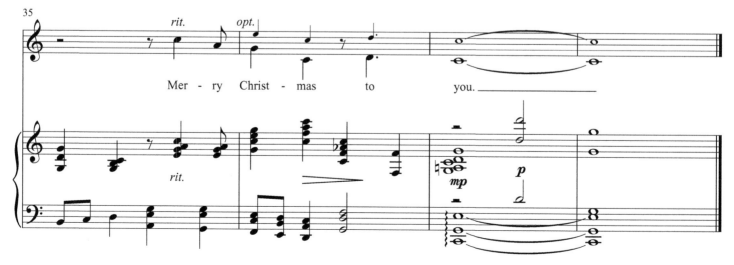

Mer - ry Christ - mas to you. __

The Christmas Waltz

Words by Sammy Cahn
Music by Jule Styne
Arranged by Hank Powell

Moderate Waltz

Frost - ed win - dow panes, _____ can - dles gleam - ing in -

side, Pain - ted can - dy canes _____ on the tree;

San - ta's on his way, he's filled his

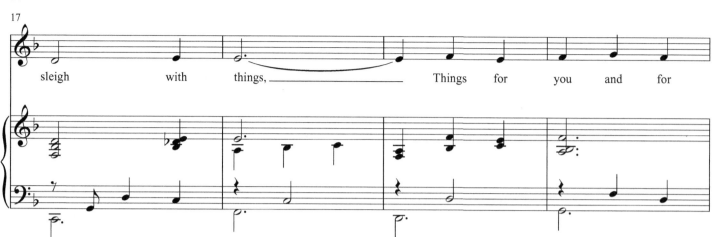

sleigh with things, _____ Things for you and for

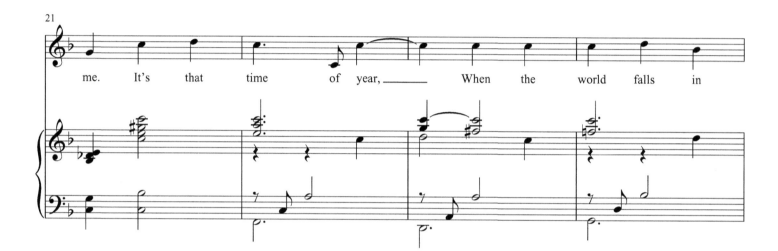

me. It's that time of year, _____ When the world falls in

love, Ev - 'ry song you hear _____ seems to say: _____

_____ "Mer - ry Christ - mas, _____ May your New Year

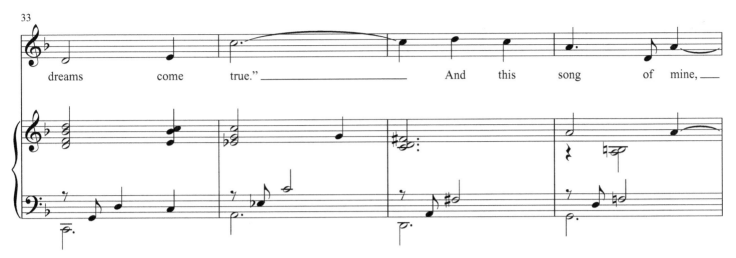

dreams come true." _____ And this song of mine, _____

_____ in three - quar - ter time, _____ Wish - es you and yours _____

Jazz Waltz

_____ the same thing too. _____

lightly

San - ta's on his way, he's filled his sleigh with

things, _____ Things for you and for me. It's

that time of year ____ when the world falls in love. Ev - 'ry

song you hear ____ seems to say: _____ "Mer - ry Christ - mas, ____

May your New Year's dreams come true." _____ And

this song of mine _____ in three quar - ter time _____

_____ wish - es you and yours the same

thing too. _____

Have Yourself a Merry Little Christmas

from MEET ME IN ST. LOUIS

Words and Music by Hugh Martin
and Ralph Blane
Arranged by Celeste Avery

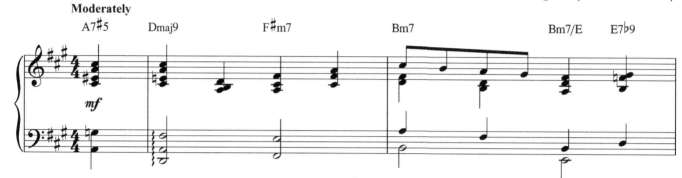

When the stee - ple bells

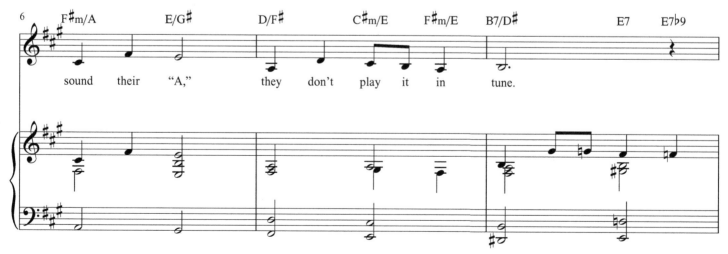

sound their "A," they don't play it in tune.

*An archaic English term for the highest celestial sphere.

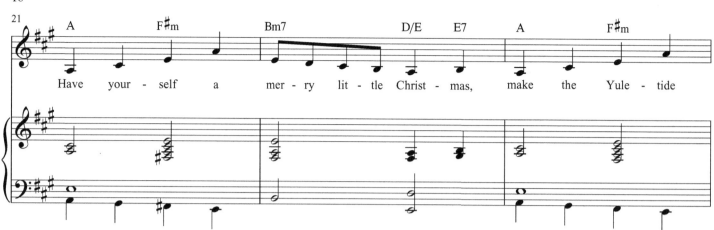

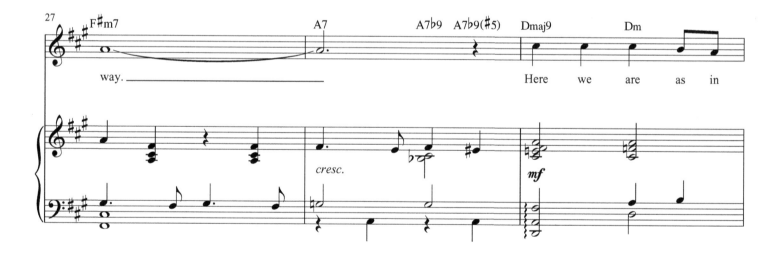

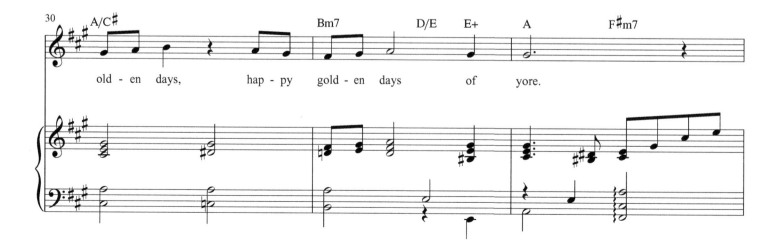

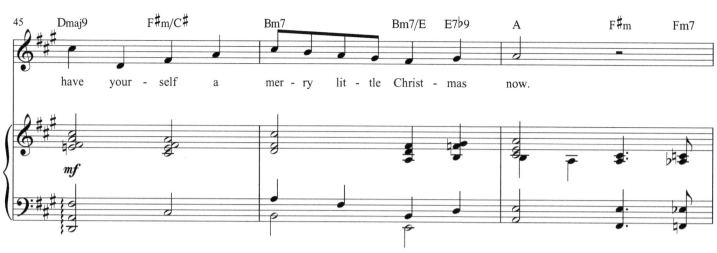

have your - self a mer - ry lit - tle Christ - mas now.

Here we are as in old - en days, hap - py

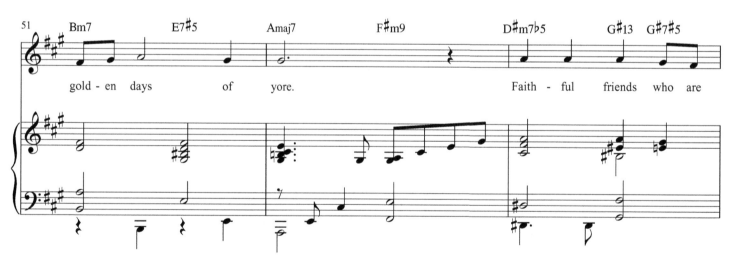

gold - en days of yore. Faith - ful friends who are

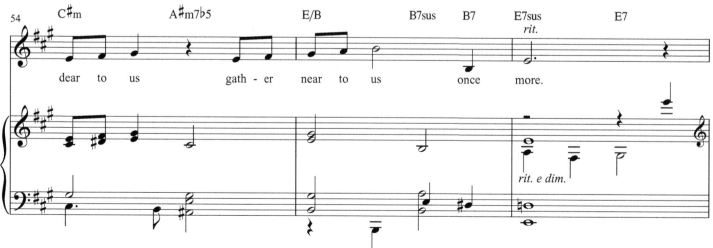

dear to us gath - er near to us once more.

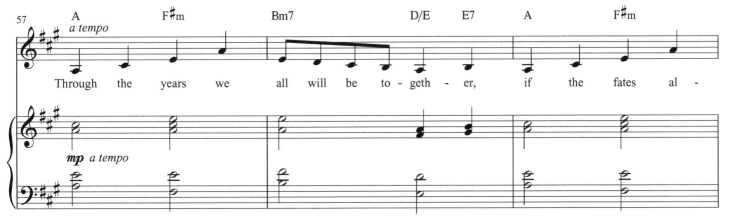

Through the years we all will be to - geth - er, if the fates al -

low.

Hang a shin - ing star up - on the high - est

Original lyric: Un - til then we'll have to mud - dle through some -

bough, _____ and

how. _____ So

have your - self a

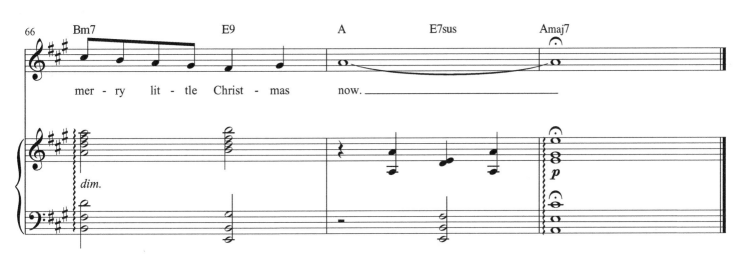

mer - ry lit - tle Christ - mas now. _____

I Wonder As I Wander
(Appalachian Carol)

By John Jacob Niles

When Mar - y birthed Je - sus, 'twas in a cow's stall, With

wise men and farm - ers and shep - herds and all. But high from God's heav - en a

star's light did fall, And the prom - ise of a - ges it then did re - call.

If Je - sus had want - ed for an - y wee thing, A

star in the sky, or a bird on the wing, Or all of God's an - gels in

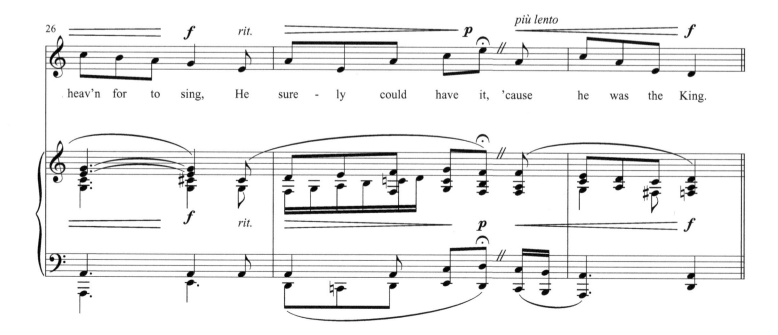

heav'n for to sing, He sure - ly could have it, 'cause he was the King.

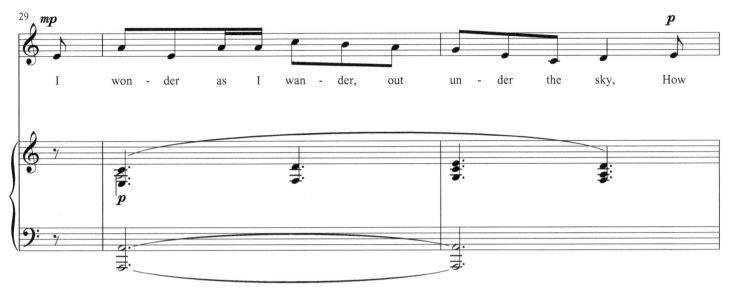

I won - der as I wan - der, out un - der the sky, How

Je - sus the Sav - ior did come for to die For poor on - 'ry peo - ple like

you and like I... I won - der as I wan - der, out un - der the sky.

I'll Be Home For Christmas

Words and Music by Kim Gannon
and Walter Kent
Arranged by Luke Duane

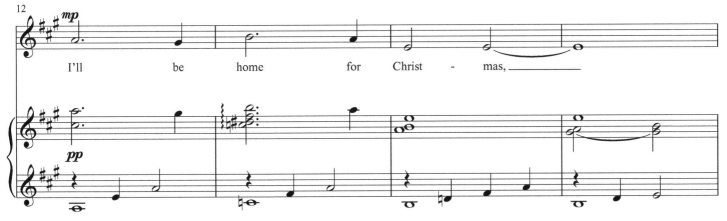

I'll be home for Christ - mas,

you can count on me.

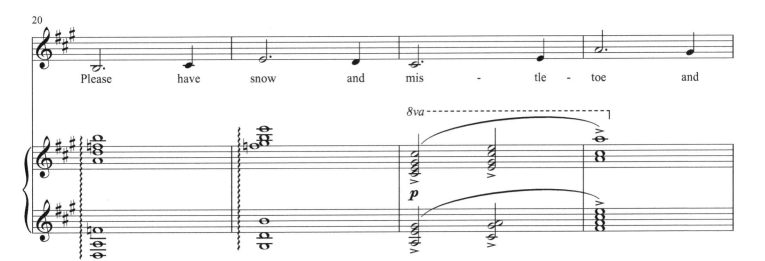

Please have snow and mis - tle - toe and

pres - ents on the tree.

Christ - mas Eve will find me _____ where the

love - light gleams. _____ I'll be

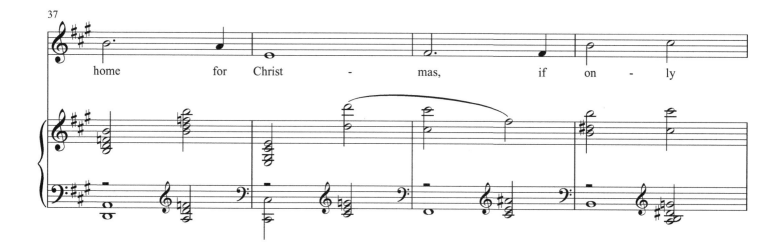

home for Christ - mas, if on - ly

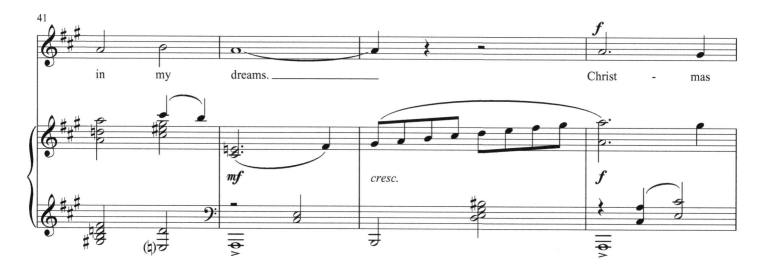

in my dreams. _____ Christ - mas

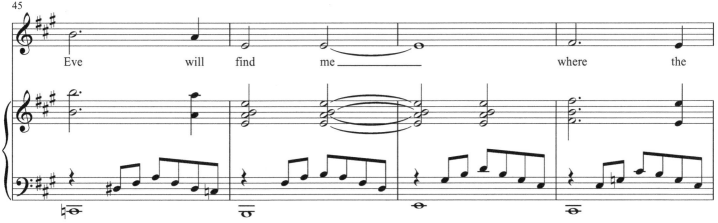

Eve will find me _____ where the

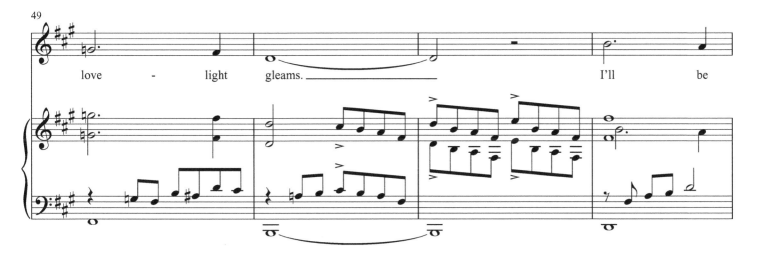

love - light gleams. _____ I'll be

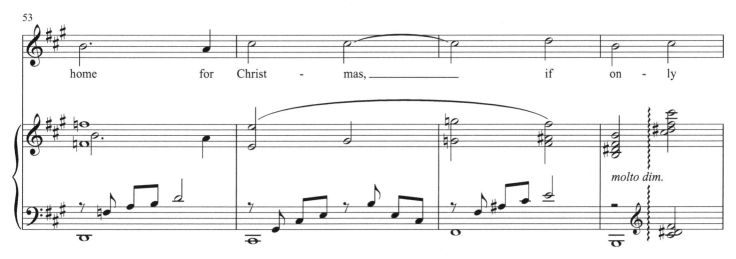

home for Christ - mas, _____ if on - ly

in my dreams. _____

In the Bleak Midwinter

Poem by Christina Georgina Rossetti
Music by Gustav Holst
Arranged by Brian Dean

In the bleak mid-win-ter, frost-y wind made moan, earth stood hard as iron, wa-ter like a stone; snow had fall-en, snow on snow,

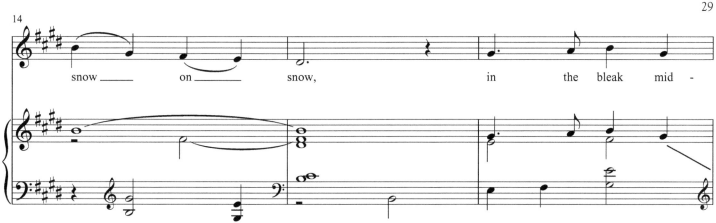

snow _____ on _____ snow, in the bleak mid -

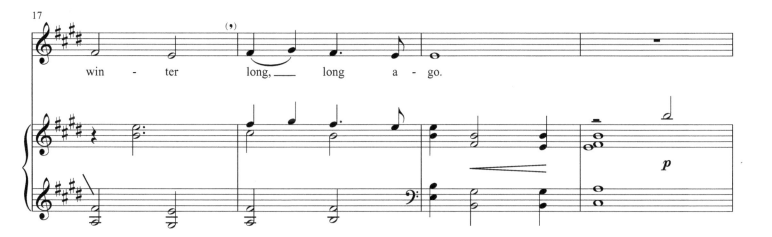

win - ter long, _____ long a - go.

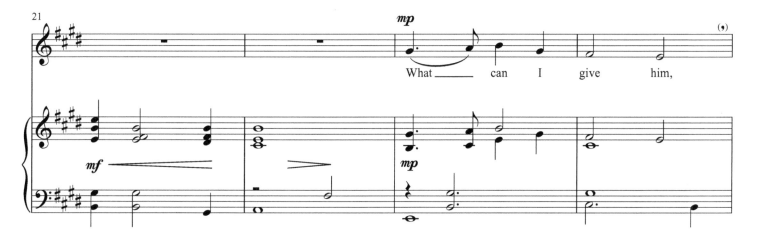

What _____ can I give him,

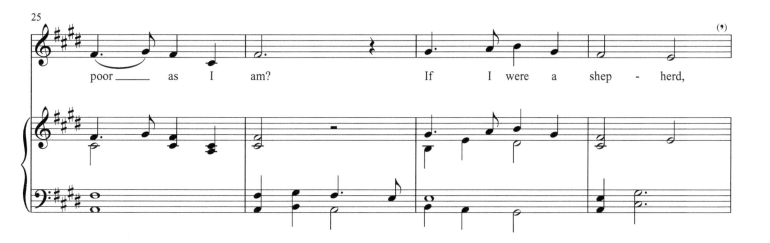

poor _____ as I am? If I were a shep - herd,

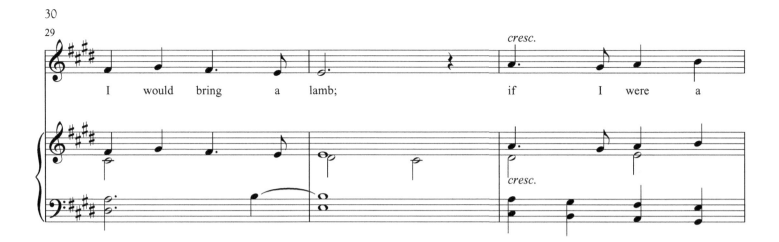

I would bring a lamb; if I were a

wise man, I would do my part; Yet what I can, I

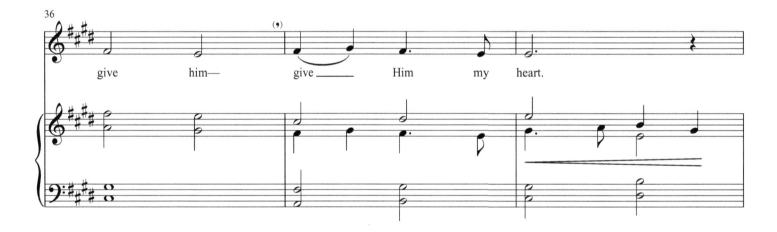

give him— give ___ Him my heart.

I would give my heart.

O Holy Night
(Cantique de Noël)

French Words by Placide Cappeau
English Words by John S. Dwight
Music by Adolphe Adam

9
pin - ing, Till he ap-peared, and the soul felt its
nel - le Et de son père ar - rê - ter le cour -

11
worth. A thrill of hope the
roux. Le mon - de en - tier tres -

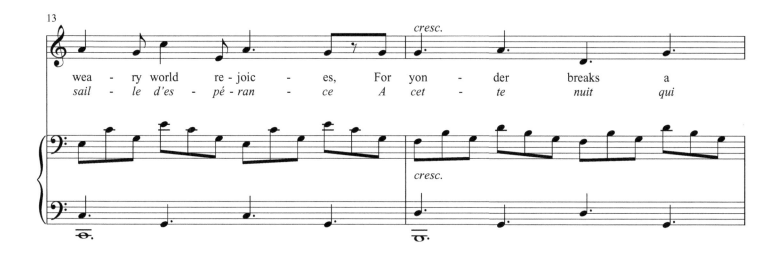

13
wea - ry world re - joic - es, For yon - der breaks a
sail - le d'es - pé - ran - ce A cet - te nuit qui

cresc.

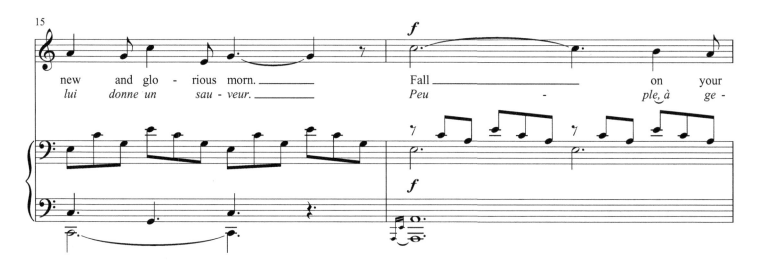

15
new and glo - rious morn. _____ Fall _____ on your
lui donne un sau - veur. _____ Peu - ple, à ge -

f

knees! _____ Oh hear _____ the an - gel
noux! _____ *at - tends* _____ *ta dé - li -*

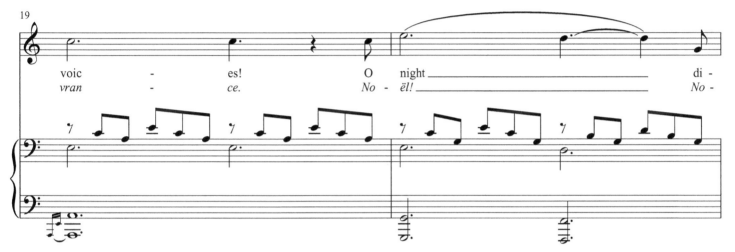

voic - es! O night _____ di -
vran - ce. No - ël! _____ *No -*

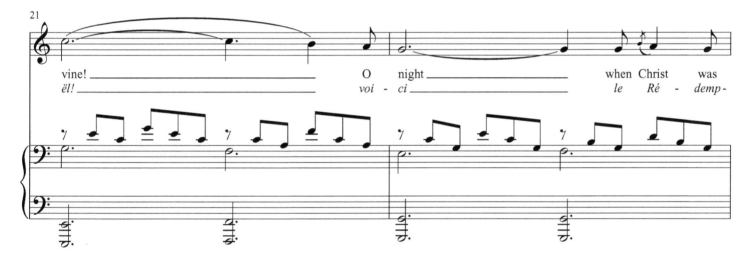

vine! _____ O night _____ when Christ was
ël! _____ *voi - ci* _____ *le Ré - demp -*

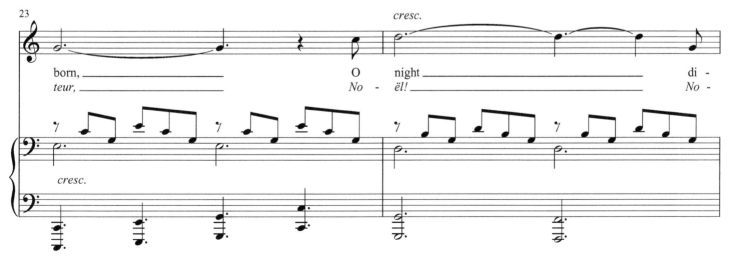

cresc.

born, _____ O night _____ di -
teur, _____ *No - ël!* _____ *No -*

cresc.

34

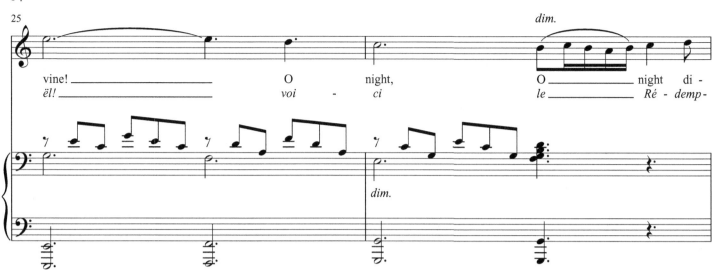

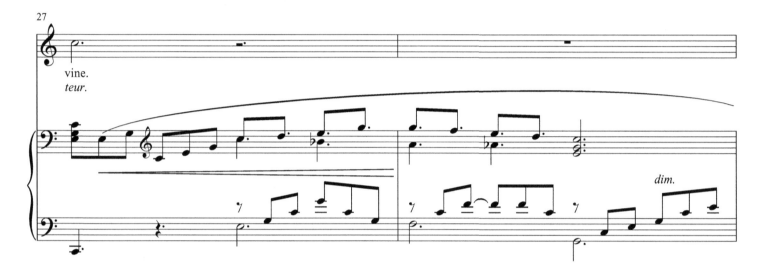

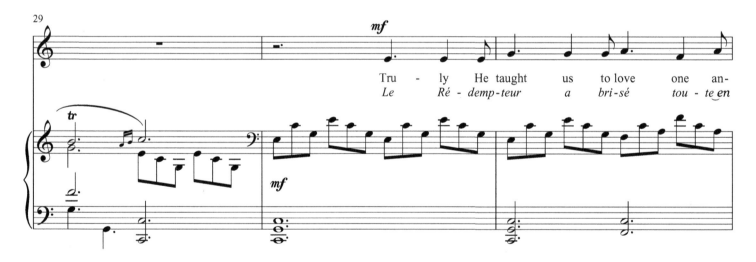

Chains shall He break, for the slave is our
Il voit un frè - re_où n'é - tait qu'un es -

broth - er, And in His name____ all op - pres - sion shall
cla - ve, L'a-mour u - nit____ ceux qu'en-chaî - nait le

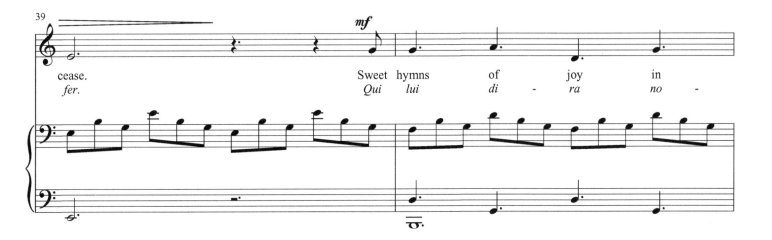

cease. Sweet hymns of joy in
fer. Qui lui di - ra no -

grate - ful cho - rus raise we, Let all with - in us
tre re - con - nais-san - ce? C'est pour nous tous qu'il

praise His Ho - ly name. _____ Christ _____ is the
naît, qu'il souf - fre et meurt. _____ Peu - ple, de -

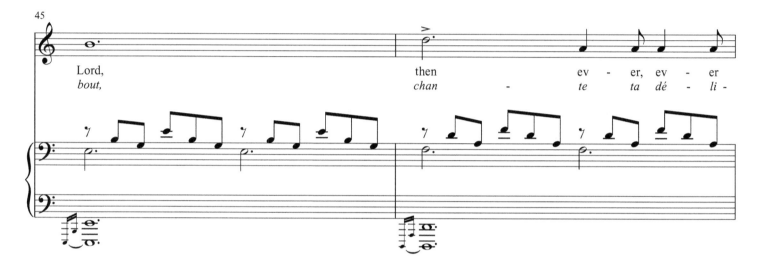

Lord, then ev - er, ev - er
bout, chan - te ta dé - li -

praise we, His pow'r _____ and
vran - ce, No - ël! _____ No -

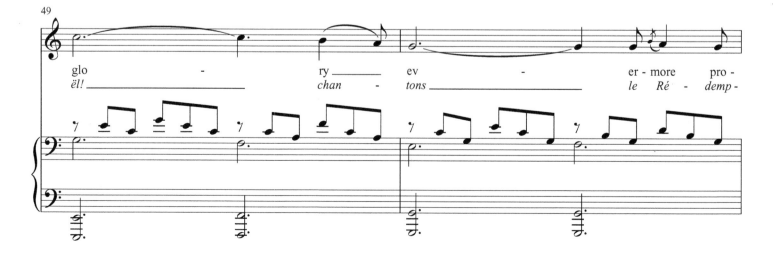

glo - ry _____ ev - er - more pro -
ël! _____ chan - tons _____ le Ré - demp -

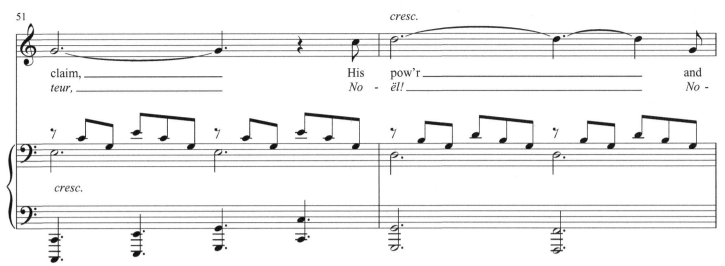

claim, _____ His pow'r _____ and
teur, _____ No - ël! _____ No -

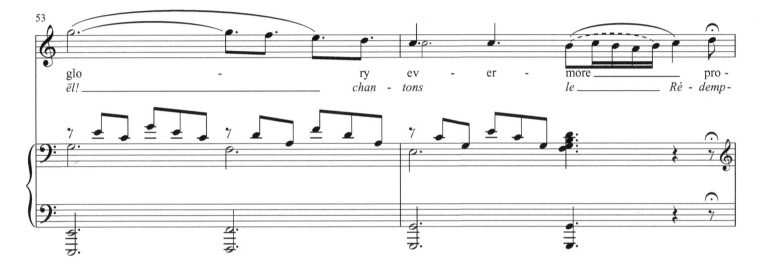

glo - ry ev - er - more _____ pro -
ël! _____ chan - tons le _____ Ré - demp -

claim.
teur.

It Came Upon the Midnight Clear

Traditional English Melody
Words by E.H. Sears
Adapted by Arthur Sullivan
Arranged by Richard Walters

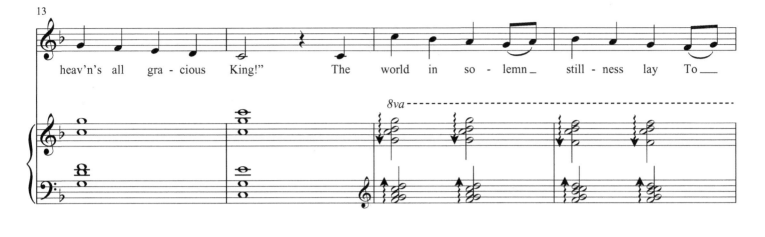

heav'n's all gra - cious King!" The world in so - lemn still - ness lay To

hear the an - gels sing. Still

through the clo - ven skies they come, With peace - ful wings un - furled; And

still their heav'n - ly mu - sic floats O'er all the wear - y world. A -

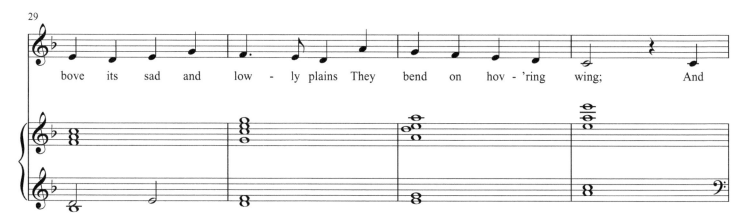

bove its sad and low - ly plains They bend on hov - 'ring wing; And

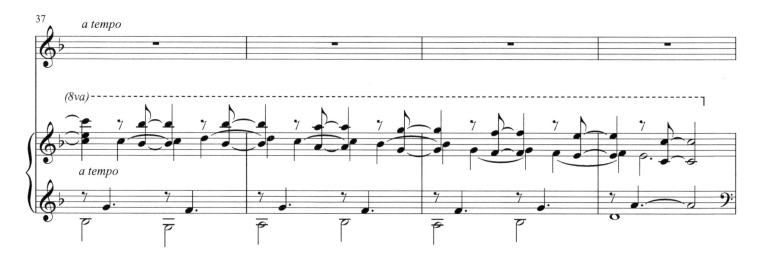

ev - er o'er its __ Ba - bel sounds, The __ bless - ed an - gels sing.

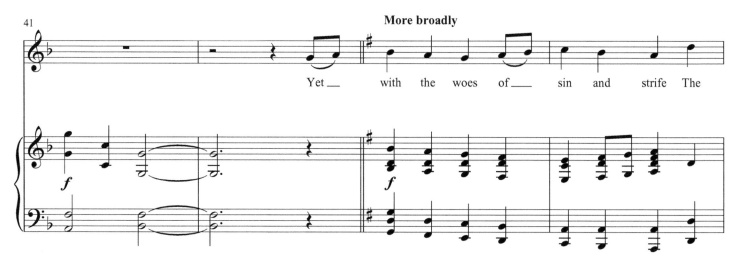

Yet __ with the woes of __ sin and strife The

world has suf - fered long; Be - neath the an - gel strain have rolled Two _

thou - sand years of wrong; And man, at war with man, hears not The

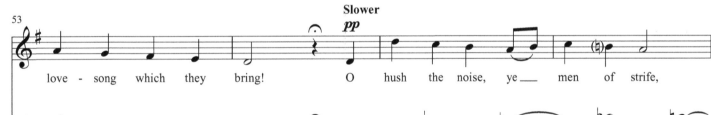

Slower

love - song which they bring! O hush the noise, ye _ men of strife,

And _ hear _ the an - gels sing.

Mary Had a Baby

African-American Spiritual
Arranged by Richard Walters

Where was he born,___ my Lord? Where was he born,___ my Lord?

Mar-y had a ba - by, born in a sta - ble. Mar-y had a ba - by, my Lord.

Laid him in a man-ger, my Lord. Laid him in a man-ger,

my Lord. Mar-y had a ba - by, laid him in a man-ger. Mar-y had a ba - by, my Lord.

The Most Wonderful Time of the Year

Words and Music by Eddie Pola
and George Wyle
Arranged by Luke Duane

tell - ing you, "Be of good cheer."_____ It's the
meet - ings, when friends come to call._____ It's the

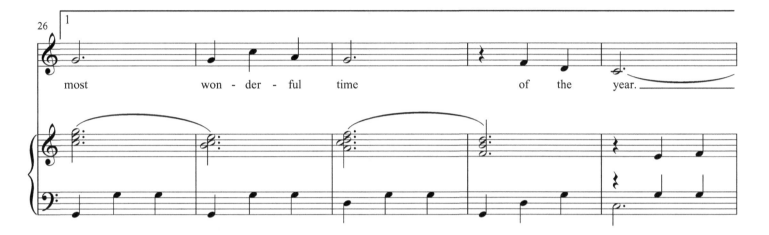

most won - der - ful time of the year._____

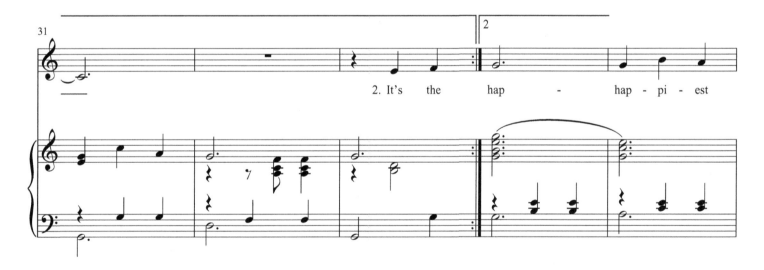

2. It's the hap - hap - pi - est

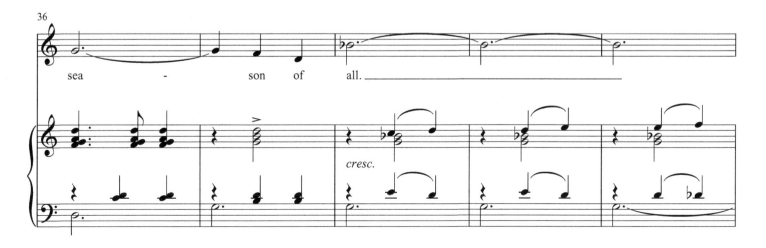

sea - son of all._____

cresc.

of the year. _____ There'll be

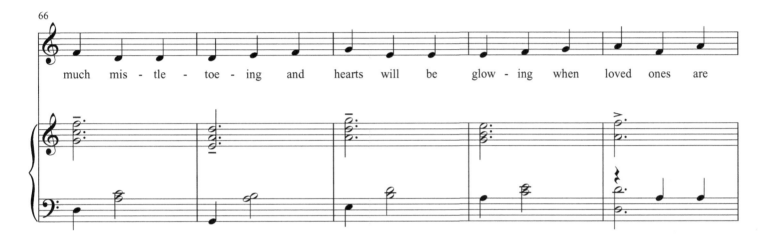

much mis - tle - toe - ing and hearts will be glow - ing when loved ones are

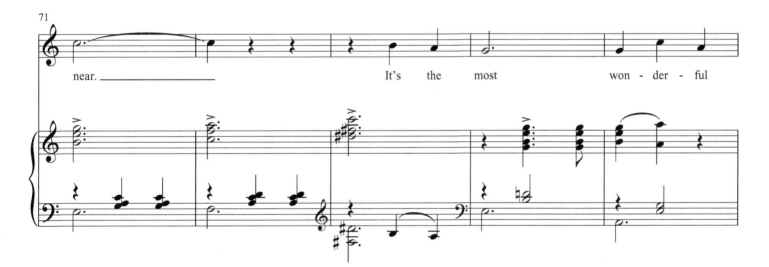

near. _____ It's the most won - der - ful

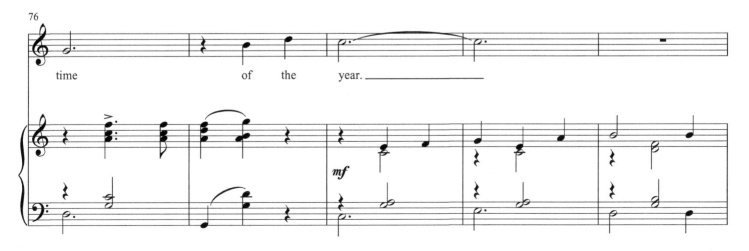

time of the year. _____

mf

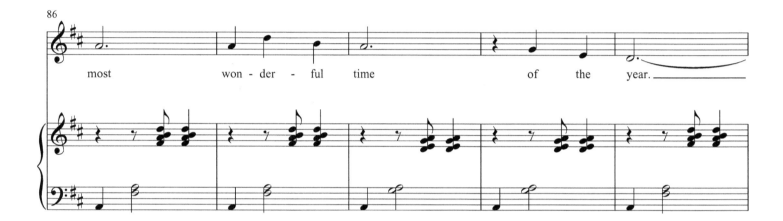

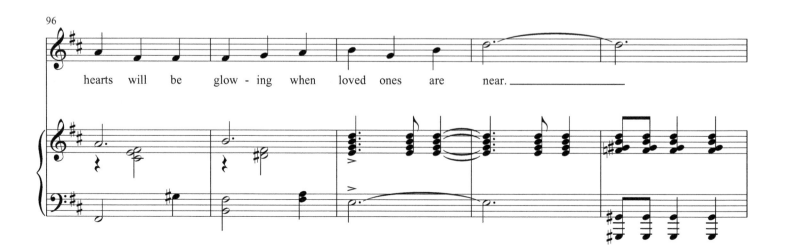

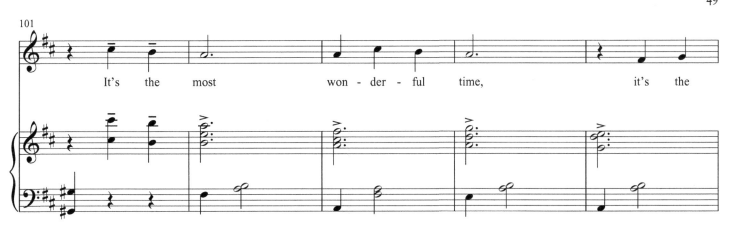

It's the most won - der - ful time, it's the

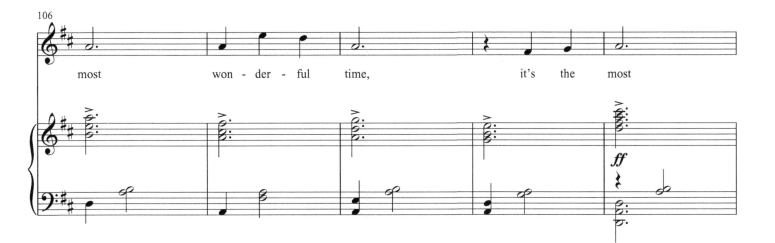

most won - der - ful time, it's the most

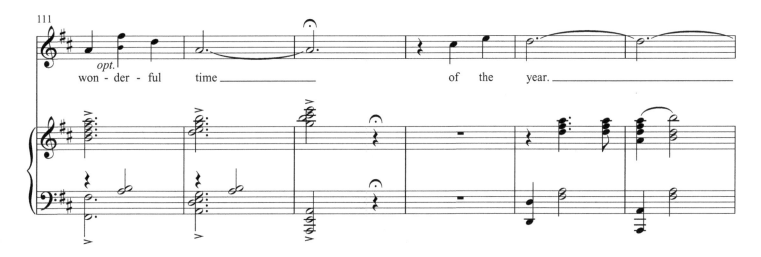

won - der - ful time _____ of the year. _____

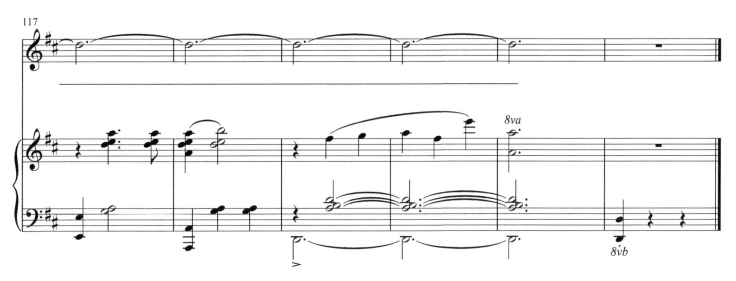

Silent Night

Words by Joseph Mohr
Translated by John F. Young
Music by Franz Xaver Gruber
Arranged by Brendan Fox

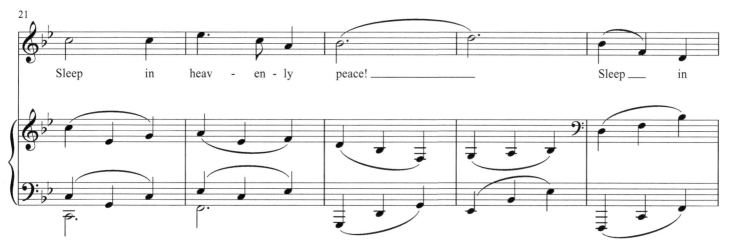

Sleep in heav - en - ly peace! _____ Sleep ___ in

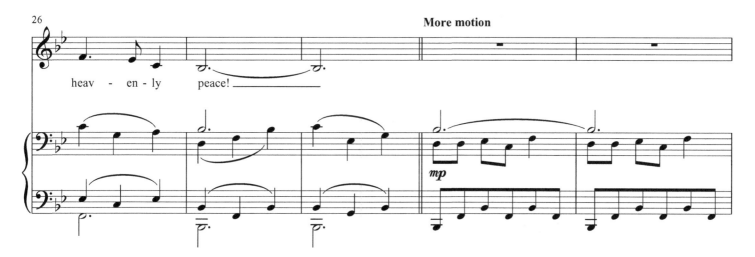

More motion

heav - en - ly peace! _____

mp

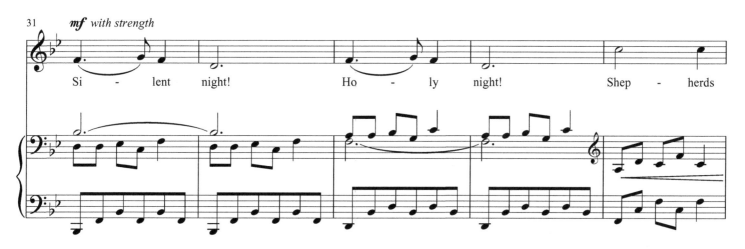

mf with strength

Si - lent night! Ho - ly night! Shep - herds

quake at the sight! Glo - ries stream ___ from

mf

Heav - en a - far, Heaven - ly hosts _____ sing Al - le - lu -

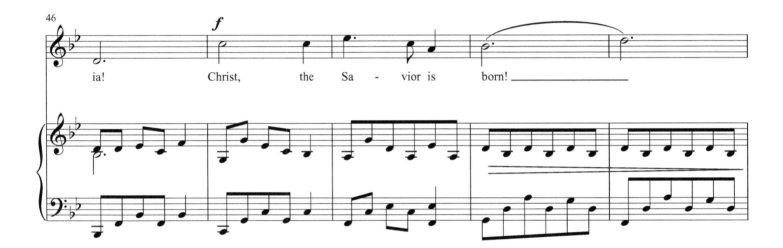

ia! Christ, the Sa - vior is born! _____

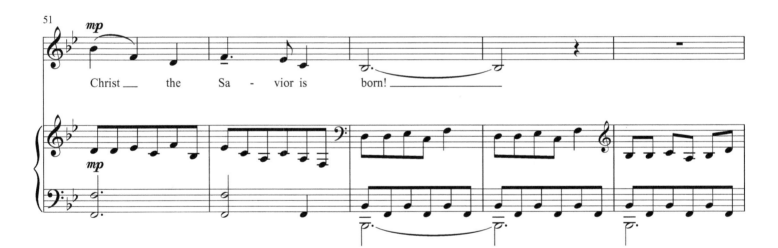

Christ ___ the Sa - vior is born! _____

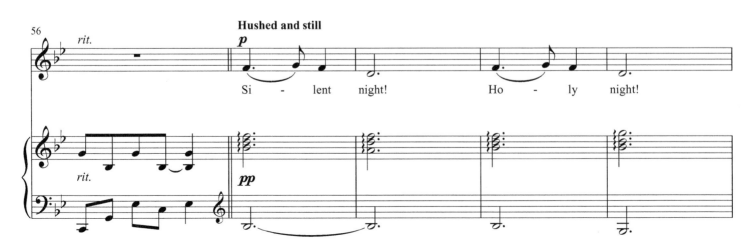

Hushed and still

Si - lent night! Ho - ly night!

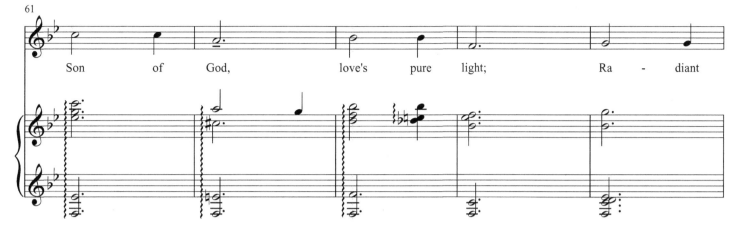

Son of God, love's pure light; Ra - diant

beams____ from Thy ho - ly face with the dawn of re -

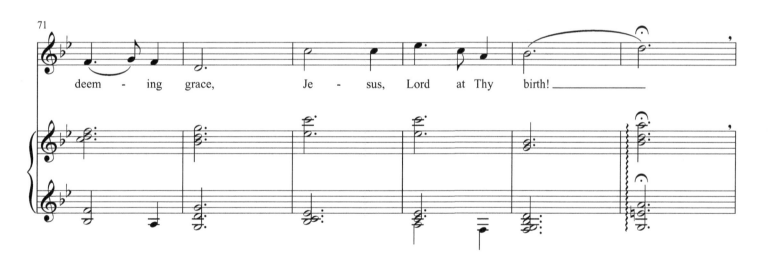

deem - ing grace, Je - sus, Lord at Thy birth!_____

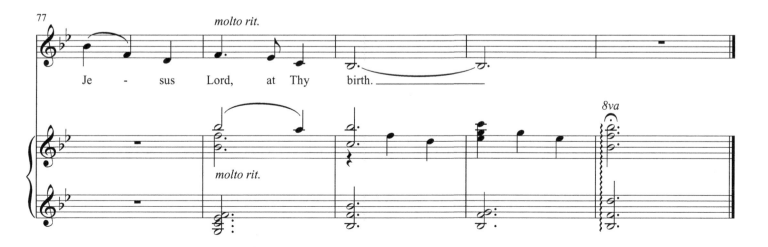

Je - sus Lord, at Thy birth._____

Silver Bells
from the Paramount Picture THE LEMON DROP KID

Words and Music by Jay Livingston
and Ray Evans
Arranged by Luke Duane

here is what Christ - mas time means to

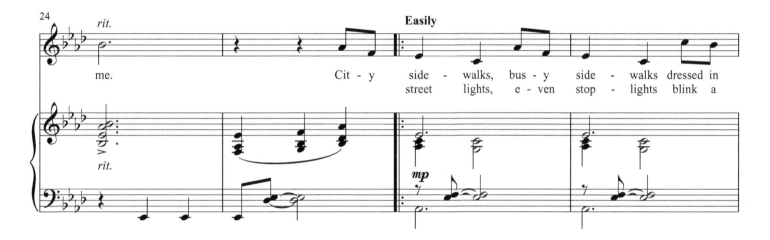

me.

rit.

Easily

Cit - y side - walks, bus - y side - walks dressed in
street lights, e - ven stop - lights blink a

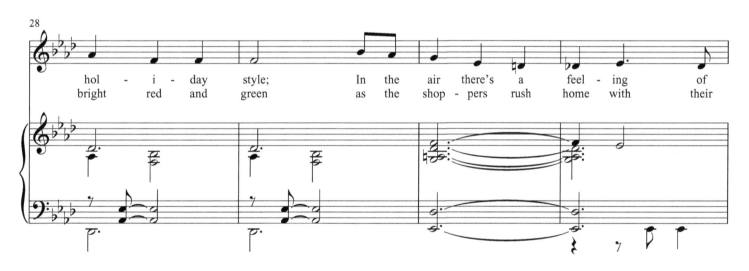

hol - i - day style; In the air there's a feel - ing of
bright red and green as the shop - pers rush home with their

Christ - mas. _____ Chil - dren laugh - ing, peo - ple pass - ing, meet - ing
treas - ures. _____ Hear the snow crunch, see the kids bunch, this is

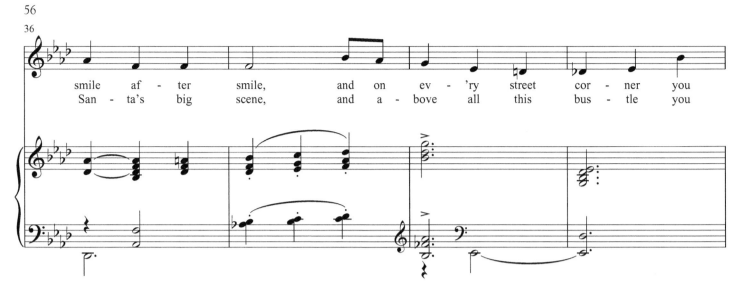

smile af - ter smile, and on ev - 'ry street cor - ner you
San - ta's big scene, and a - bove all this bus - tle you

hear: _____
hear: _____

Sil - ver bells, _____

8va (both hands)

cresc.

mf

p

p

sil - ver bells, _____ it's Christ - mas

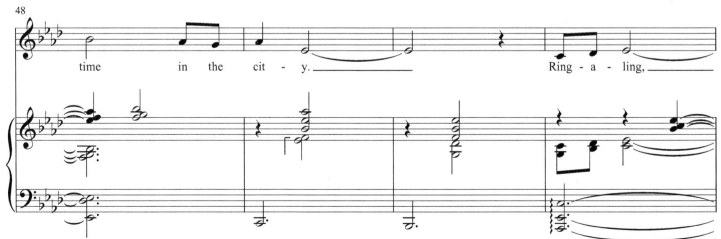

time in the cit - y. _____ Ring - a - ling, _____

This page has intentionally been left blank to facilitate page turns.

Sleigh Ride

Music by Leroy Anderson
Words by Mitchell Parish
Arranged by Celeste Avery

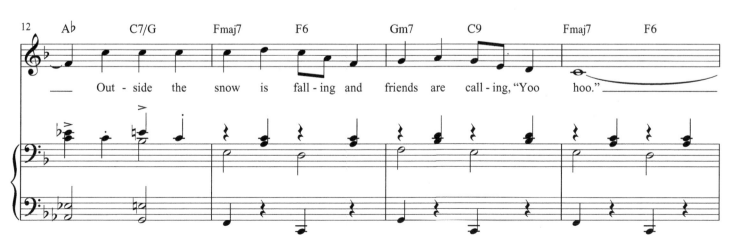

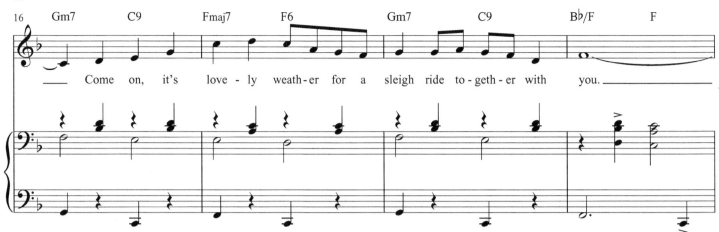

Come on, it's love-ly weath-er for a sleigh ride to-geth-er with you. _____

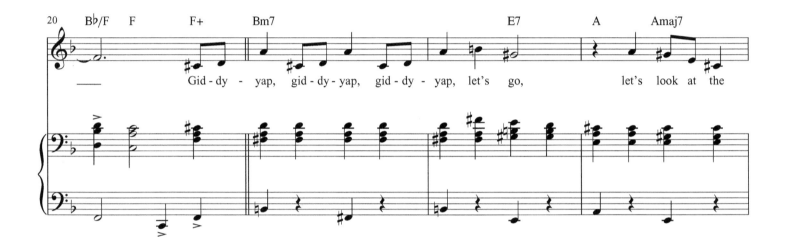

_____ Gid-dy - yap, gid-dy-yap, gid-dy - yap, let's go, let's look at the

show. We're rid-ing in a won-der-land of snow. _____

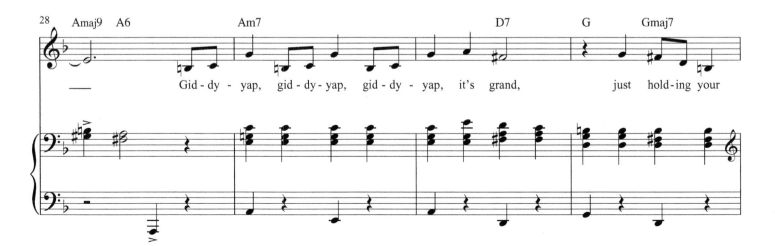

_____ Gid-dy - yap, gid-dy-yap, gid-dy - yap, it's grand, just hold-ing your

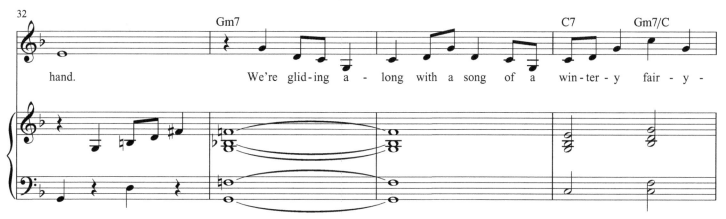

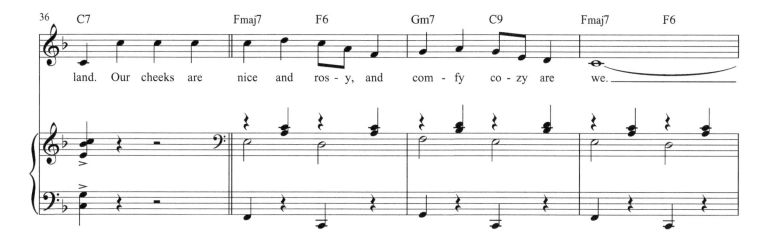

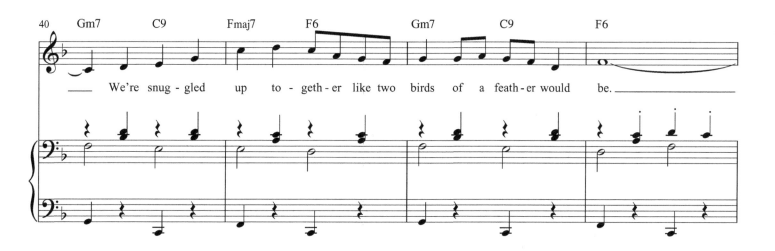

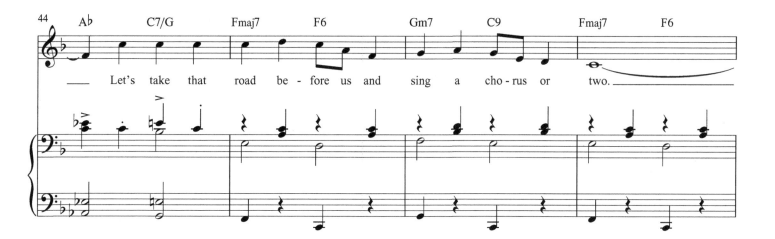

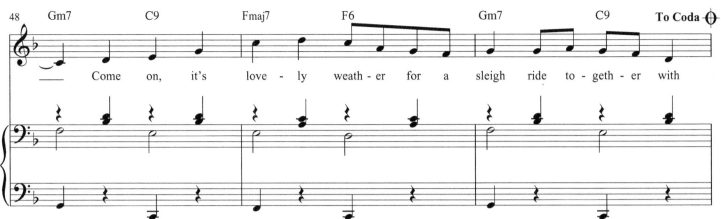

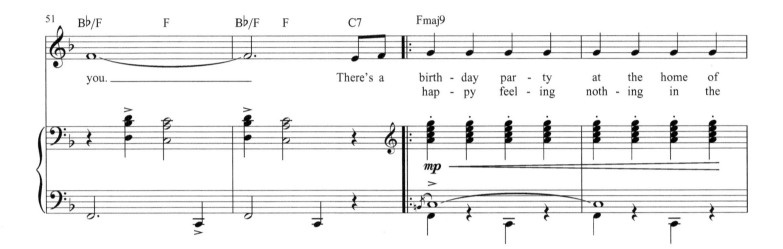

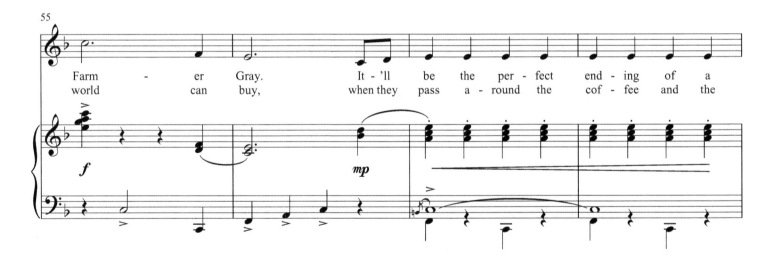

White Christmas
from the Motion Picture Irving Berlin's HOLIDAY INN

Words and Music by
Irving Berlin
Arranged by Richard Walters

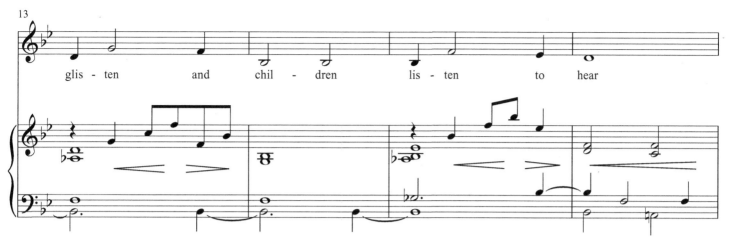

glis - ten and chil - dren lis - ten to hear

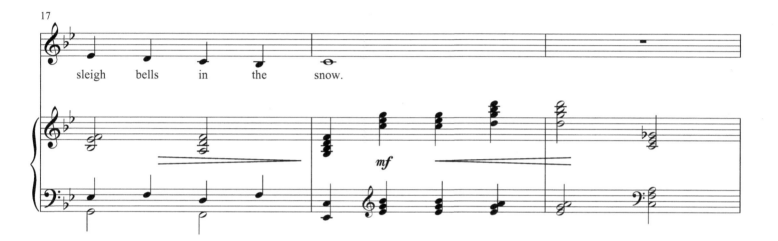

sleigh bells in the snow.

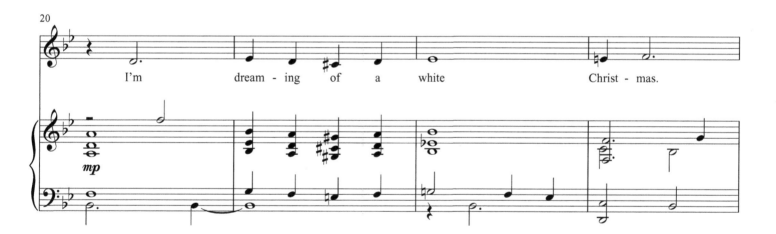

I'm dream - ing of a white Christ - mas.

With ev - 'ry Christ - mas card I write: "May your

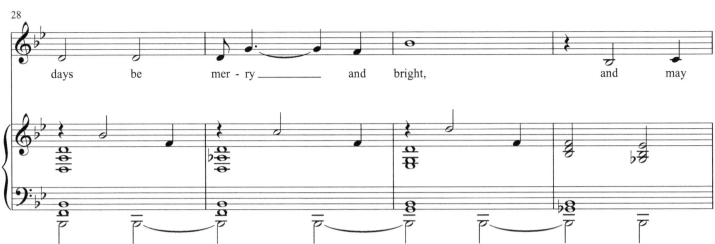

days be mer - ry _____ and bright, and may

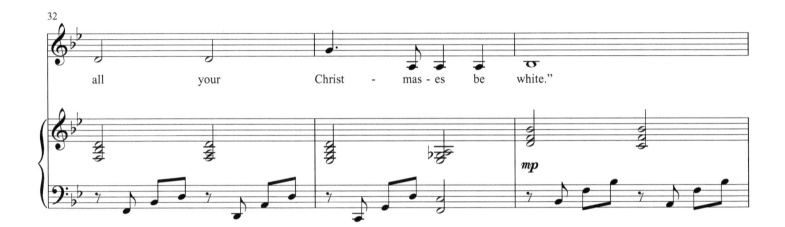

all your Christ - mas - es be white."

I'm dream - ing of a

white Christ - mas. With ev - 'ry

Christ - mas card I write:

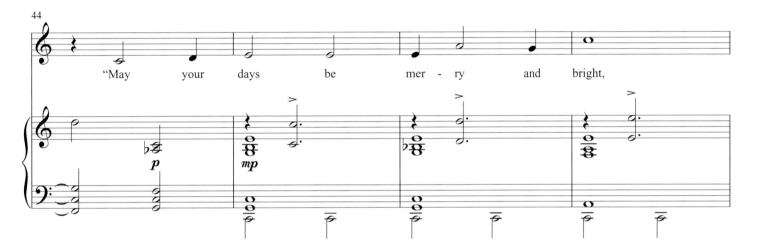

"May your days be mer - ry and bright,

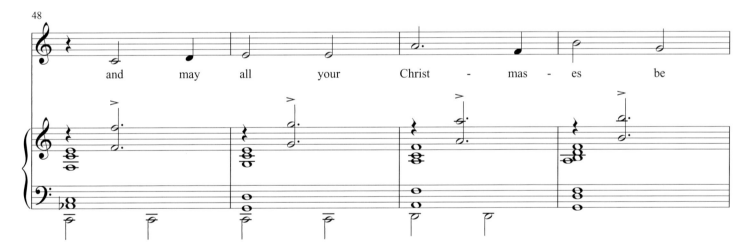

and may all your Christ - mas - es be

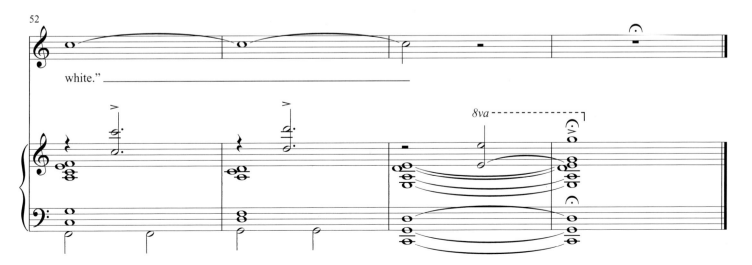

white."